BASIC CRYPTO TRADING FOR BEGINNER KIDS

Unlocking the Secrets of Cryptocurrency Trading and Investment for Smart Young Investors

James Vega

TABLE OF CONTENT

Part One: Crypto Craze Crash Course

Chapter One

What is Crypto? The Secret to Financial Success in the Digital Age!

Hello there, you young man who is on the verge of becoming a money-master! We would like to take this opportunity to welcome you to the fascinating world of cryptocurrencies, where you will find a new sort of treasure: digital coins that have the potential to unlock your future luck! We are not talking about hidden chests or pirate's riches; rather, we are talking about Bitcoin, Ethereum, and a very large number of other digital currencies that are now residing on the internet!

First things first: before you start hunting for these gems, let's figure out what this "crypto" business is all about. Consider money to be a private club, where only members are permitted to utilize it. In the process of managing the flow of money, traditional banks and governments play the role of bouncers. But crypto? It is comparable to a hidden clubhouse that is constructed on a technology known as blockchain, which is a very secure internet network that prevents any bouncer (or villain!) from tampering with your belongings.

Think of the blockchain as a large public ledger, available for everyone to view. Every time you purchase or sell a cryptocurrency, it's like putting your name and the amount in this ledger. Nobody can remove it, and everyone can see it, making it incredibly secure and transparent. So, no more worries about losing your piggy bank beneath the sofa or a sly sibling taking your money!

Now, let's meet some of the interesting characters in this digital clubhouse:

- ☐ Bitcoin: The OG of crypto, like the first child on the playground who began the entire money-trading thing. Everyone knows its name, and it's very valuable (think nice footwear or that fantastic video game you've been admiring!).
- ☐ Ethereum: Bitcoin's closest buddy (sometimes competitor), but with a nifty superpower — it can execute programs and things within the blockchain! Imagine

playing mini-games or even generating your cryptocurrencies on Ethereum!

- ☐ Dogecoin: The lively dog of the crypto pack, began as a joke but is now worth more than your favorite plush animal! It's a reminder that anything can happen in the crypto realm.

And these are only a few! There are dozens of different cryptocurrencies, each with its distinct purpose and narrative. It's like collecting Pokémon cards, except instead of capturing mystical animals, you're gathering digital money with the potential to expand your riches (with Mom and Dad's aid, of course!).

But why is crypto so special? Here are some reasons:

- It's secure: The blockchain protects your funds safe from evil criminals, like a super-strong vault in the skies.

- It's fast: Sending crypto across the globe is like sending a text message — quick and simple!

- It's global: No matter where you are, you can use crypto to purchase products online or even transfer money to pals in other countries.

- It's controlled by you: Unlike conventional banks, nobody can freeze your crypto or tell you what to do with it. You're the ruler of your own digital money!

Now, before you jump off and start trading like a crazy hatter, know this: crypto is like a wild roller coaster ride. Prices may swing up and down quicker than a cheetah on a sugar high. So, it's crucial to learn the ropes, be responsible, and always trade with the guidance of trustworthy individuals.

This is only the first step in your crypto journey! In the upcoming chapters, we'll go further into how to trade, invest, and become a knowledgeable youthful investor in the digital age. So, buckle up, put on your thinking hat, and get ready to learn the amazing world of crypto!

Bonus Round:

Can you think of any more real-life instances of how blockchain technology is applied outside cryptocurrency?

Imagine you could build your cryptocurrency. What would you name it and what function would it have?

The future of finance is in your hands, young crypto champion! Keep studying, and investigating, and remember, the most precious thing you have is your curiosity and excitement to uncover the world of digital riches!

Chapter Two

Meet the Crypto Crew: Exploring Popular Coins and Their Cool Powers

Hey there, young crypto cadets! Are you ready to meet the trendiest bunch on the digital block? In this chapter, we're focusing on some of the most recognized faces in the cryptocurrency industry, those flashy digital coins everyone's screaming about. Buckle up, because we're about to go on a fascinating tour of their abilities, idiosyncrasies, and secret skills!

- Bitcoin: The OG Crypto Captain

Imagine a pirate captain, but instead of a ship, he travels the high seas of finance on a gigantic golden Bitcoin. That's the attitude of Bitcoin, the granddaddy of all cryptocurrencies. Launched in 2009, it set the door for this entire digital gold rush, and it's still the king of the castle with its restricted supply and great value. Think of it as the strongest protection in your crypto armory, a trustworthy partner on your trading adventure.

- Ethereum: The Tech-Savvy Wizard

While Bitcoin is brawn, Ethereum is intelligence. This cryptocurrency isn't just about buying and selling; it's an entire platform where you can construct fun things like applications, games, and even your digital pets! Think of it as a magic wand that converts thoughts into reality in the crypto realm. It's also home to NFTs, those unique digital treasures everyone's talking about, making it a desirable place for creative minds and inventors.

- Dogecoin: The Meme-ing Marvel

Forget diamonds, Dogecoin shines with the power of memes! This adorable pup-themed currency began as a joke but rapidly became a favored underdog in the crypto race. Its whimsical appeal and modest price make it excellent for dipping your toes into the trading pool without jeopardizing a king's ransom. Just remember, with Dogecoin, it's more about the pleasure and community than the huge cash.

- Litecoin: The Speedy Silver Surfer

Think of Bitcoin as a ponderous tank and Litecoin as its sleek, fast relative. This silver bullet of a currency employs a different technology than Bitcoin, making it speedier and cheaper for transactions. Imagine transferring money to your buddies across the world in a blink, that's the wonder of Litecoin! It's an excellent solution for regular crypto usage and learning the ropes of trading without the expensive fees.

- Tether: The Stablecoin Anchor

While the crypto sea might be turbulent, Tether is the anchor keeping everything stable. This currency is tied to the US dollar, so its value remains about the same, unlike the ups and downs of other cryptocurrencies. Think of it as a safe harbor amid the storm, a place to deposit your gains when things get a little too crazy.

And the Crew Keeps Growing!

There are hundreds, maybe even thousands, of more interesting cryptocurrencies out there, each with its unique narrative and abilities. We've only met a handful of the most popular ones, but remember, the crypto world is continuously developing, and new members join the team all the time! Keep your eyes out for up-and-coming stars and study before you buy.

Remember, Young Investors:

- Every coin has its strengths and disadvantages. Do your study before picking one to invest in.
- Diversify your portfolio: Don't put all your eggs in one crypto basket!
- Never invest more than you can afford to lose, crypto may be volatile.
- Have fun and learn as you go! The crypto world is a fascinating journey, so enjoy the trip!

With this information under your belt, you're ready to go further into the world of each cryptocurrency. Explore their websites, join online groups, and learn everything you can about their unique characteristics and possibilities. Remember, information is power, and in the crypto world, it's the key to unlocking fantastic possibilities!

And that's all for now, future crypto lords! Go out and discover the vast and exciting world of the Crypto Crew. Just remember, safety first, pleasure always, and keep learning new things every day! The future of money is in your hands, so make it a great experience!

Chapter Three

Trading Terms to Tame: Demystifying Crypto Jargon Like a Pro!

Hey there again, young crypto explorers! Welcome to Chapter 3, where we'll equip you with the hidden language of crypto trading. No need for expensive decoder rings or Morse code abilities; we're breaking down that difficult terminology so you can communicate with seasoned traders like a champ! Buckle up, future financial whizzes, it's time to master the trading jargon jungle!

First Stop: Market Mavens

Let's start with the basics: purchasing and selling. Think of it like swapping your old video game for a new one. You purchase the new game (cryptocurrency) if you believe it'll be worth more later, like catching a rare Pokémon! When you sell the game (cryptocurrency), you cash in on its increasing worth, exactly like trading in your collection for the newest console. Easy, right?

Now, how do you determine when to purchase or sell? That's where holding comes in. If you trust in a cryptocurrency's future, you could hang it onto it, like preserving your favorite baseball card because you know it'll be valuable later. But remember, the crypto market may be like a rollercoaster, so holding isn't always plain sailing!

Understanding the Market's Roar: Market Cap and Volatility

Imagine a huge piggy bank stocked with all the digital pennies in the globe. That's what market capitalization (market cap) is! The larger the piggy bank, the more precious the bitcoin. Bitcoin, for example, has a vast piggy bank, making it like the king of the crypto jungle.

But things can become crazy in the crypto realm, with values bouncing up and down quicker than a kangaroo! That's where volatility comes in. Think of it as the market's mood swings. A highly volatile crypto may change value like a chameleon shifting colors, whereas a less volatile one is more relaxed, like your friendly neighborhood sloth. Understanding volatility helps you determine how daring you want to be with your trading selections.

Keeping Your Coins Cozy: Wallets and Security

Remember your piggy bank with your treasured allowance? Imagine a digital piggy bank for your coins. That's a wallet! There are numerous sorts of wallets, from ones on your phone or PC to elegant hardware wallets that look like small treasure chests. Choosing the correct wallet is like finding the ideal hiding hole for your birthday money — safe and secure!

Speaking of security, it's time to harness your inner ninja! Protecting your crypto is like keeping your hidden fort from sneaky ninjas. Use secure passwords, keep your wallet software updated, and never disclose your private keys (consider them as the ultimate fort codes) with anybody!

Trading Terms Glossary:

- Buying: Acquiring bitcoin in exchange for another currency (typically fiat like dollars).
- Selling: Exchanging your Bitcoin for another currency, preferably at a profit!
- Holding: Keeping your cryptocurrency instead of selling it, expecting its value would improve.
- Market Cap: The total worth of all outstanding coins of a given cryptocurrency.
- Volatility: The degree to which the price of a cryptocurrency moves up and down.

- Wallet: A safe digital storage method for your cryptocurrency.

Mission Accomplished!

There you have it, little cryptonauts! You've tamed the trading terminology jungle, equipped with the knowledge to navigate the thrilling world of crypto. Remember, practice makes perfect (and money!), so keep learning, have fun, and always trade wisely.

Bonus Quest: Now that you understand these concepts, try utilizing them in a conversation with your friends! See who can construct the most epic crypto trading narrative!

Good luck, young investors! The future of finance awaits!

Chapter Four

Tech Tools for Tiny Traders: Mastering the Marketplace

Welcome back, young crypto crusaders, to the leading edge of your financial future! In this chapter, we'll dig into the tech toolbox that unlocks the intriguing world of Bitcoin trading. Forget convoluted spreadsheets and obscure code — we're talking user-friendly exchanges and applications, meant to make trading as fluid as your favorite video game.

Think of an exchange as your virtual marketplace for buying and selling Bitcoin. Imagine a digital market where you may explore various cryptocurrency booths, compare pricing, and make your first transactions. But before you unleash your inner Warren Buffet, let's investigate some kid-friendly options:

1. The Exchange Playground:

- Coinbase: Picture a bright, straightforward site suitable for newcomers. It's like the training ground for little giants, providing big cryptos like Bitcoin and Ethereum, with straightforward buy-and-sell buttons and useful instructional tools.

- Gemini: Think of Gemini as your trusty elder sister in the crypto realm. It emphasizes on security and user-friendliness, delivering a simple interface and straightforward costs.

- Binance Junior (Coming Soon!): Calling all future crypto kings and queens! Binance is building a customized platform made specifically for you, complete with instructional activities and a simpler trading experience. Stay tuned for this amazing launch!

2. App Attack! Trading on the Go:

- Spark: Imagine maintaining your Bitcoin portfolio like a pocket monster collection. Spark gamifies the experience, allowing you to acquire and trade over 50 cryptos with entertaining incentives and a vivid interface.

- Piggybank: This app's name tells it all! Piggybank enables you to invest in crypto with leftover change, rounding up your ordinary purchases and converting them into digital riches over time.

- Bits of Gold: Want to learn while you trade? Bits of Gold rewards you with educational quizzes and activities for every transaction, converting crypto into a treasure hunt for information.

3. Setting Sail in to Your Secure Account:

Now, let's build up your crypto sanctuary! Remember, safety is our password. Here's what to do:

- Choose a Strong Password: Think of it like your own fort key. Avoid popular terms or birthdays, and make a combination of uppercase and lowercase characters, numerals, and symbols. Mom

and Dad may help you remember it
securely.

- Two-Factor Authentication (2FA): This is
  like constructing a moat around your
  fortress. Enable 2FA to get a secret code
  on your phone every time you log in,
  making it incredibly challenging for
  intruders to enter.

- Store Your Coins Wisely: Think of a
  digital wallet as your treasure chest. Don't
  store your crypto on the exchange, since
  it's like leaving your gold coins lying
  about. Choose a trusted cold wallet, a safe
  device that holds your funds offline, like a
  high-tech piggy bank.

Bonus Tip: Remember, Mom and Dad are your financial co-pilots on this adventure. Always engage them in setting up your account and trading selections. Their counsel and assistance are your most essential assets!

With your exchange picked, app downloaded, and account protected, you're ready to take your first steps into the crypto market. Remember, learning and exploration are vital. Be patient, ask questions, and don't be afraid to make errors — that's how you learn as a trader. So, young investors, strap up, open your applications, and be ready to navigate the thrilling world of cryptocurrencies with confidence and knowledge!

Part Two: Trading Tactics for Tiny Titans

Chapter Five

Buy Low, Sell High (But Wait!): Mastering the Market Moves

Imagine yourself as a pirate commander, navigating the stormy waters of the Bitcoin market. Your ship is your crypto wealth, stocked with digital valuables like Bitcoin and Ethereum.

Your goal? To traverse the waves of price shifts, purchase when the seas are calm and prices are low, and then sell when the winds of opportunity fill your sails, sending your gains flying into the sky. Sounds interesting, right? But before you set to ship, there are several critical fundamentals any new crypto pirate has to master.

Part 1: Charting the Course: Reading the Market's Waves

Just as pirates depend on weather charts and stars to navigate, crypto traders utilize charts to analyze market movements. Think of a chart as a map of the sea, with each point reflecting the price of a coin at a certain moment. You'll witness mountains (high prices) and valleys (low prices), waves (short-term swings), and even tsunamis (large, rapid shifts). Learning to "read" these charts can help you forecast the moves of the market and make educated choices about buying and selling.

Here are some crucial words to gain your bearings:

- Trend: The general direction of the market — is it moving up (bullish) or down (bearish)?

- Support and Resistance: These are lines on the chart that behave as "floors" and "ceilings" for the price. When the price drops below a support line, it can be a good moment to purchase. When it meets a resistance line, it could be time to sell.

- Indicators: These are instruments that study the chart and attempt to anticipate future moves. Some prominent indicators are the Moving Average Convergence Divergence (MACD) and the Relative Strength Index (RSI).

Remember, charting is not a crystal ball, and forecasting the future is tough even for seasoned pirates. But learning how to read the market will give you a leg up in the trading game.

Part 2: Setting Sail: Buy and Sell Orders Like Anchors and Sails

Now that you know the lay of the land, it's time to learn how to maneuver your ship. This is where buy and sell orders come in. These are instructions you send to the exchange, informing it what you want to do with your crypto.

Here are the basic sorts of orders:

- Market Order: This is like instructing your crew to purchase or sell your treasure as rapidly as can, at whatever the current price is. It's fantastic for quickness, but you may not obtain the greatest pricing.

- Limit Order: This is like giving your staff a set price objective. You advise them to purchase only if the price falls below a specific level (buy order) or to sell only if the price rises above a certain level (sell order). This provides you greater control over your transactions, but it could take longer to be filled if the price doesn't reach your objective.

- Stop-Loss Order: This is like creating a safety net for your ship. You instruct the exchange to automatically sell your treasure if the price goes below a specific threshold, to avoid you from losing too much if the market unexpectedly declines.

Remember, picking the proper sequence relies on the scenario and your trading objectives.

Experiment with various sorts of orders and find what works best for you.

Part 3: Avoiding the Kraken: Common Trading Pitfalls

Every pirate worth his salt has fought a few krakens in their time. In the crypto realm, these krakens are the usual dangers that might sink your ship and drain your riches. Here are a few to look out for:

- FOMO (Fear of Missing Out): Don't allow the enthusiasm and excitement of the market to cloud your judgment. Remember, purchasing simply because everyone else is buying is a recipe for catastrophe. Stick to your trading strategy and don't be scared to skip out on a fast buck if it doesn't seem right.

- FUD (Fear, Uncertainty, and Doubt): Negativity can spread like wildfire in the crypto community. Don't worry every time you hear a nasty rumor or the price lowers. Do your research and make educated judgments based on facts, not feelings.

- Overtrading: Don't be tempted to tamper with your portfolio every five minutes. Making too many transactions might eat into your earnings via fees and raise your chance of making errors. Be patient and let your strategy play out.

- Chasing Losses: Never attempt to "catch a falling knife" by putting additional money at a lost deal. If you made a mistake, accept it and move on. Trying to pursue your losses will only make things worse.

Remember, bitcoin trading is a marathon, not a sprint. Learn from your errors, keep your emotions in control, and stick to your goal. With practice and patience, you

Chapter Six

Charting the Course: Decoding the Secrets of Candlesticks and Trend Lines

Hey crypto adventurers! Welcome to chapter 6, where we'll discover the hidden language of the market: charting! No, not painting funny faces on graphs (although that's fun too), but comprehending the patterns and messages concealed inside those colorful candlesticks and enigmatic lines. Fear not, young investors, by the conclusion of this chapter, you'll be reading the market like a pro!

Imagine the stock market as a big rollercoaster: sometimes it zooms up, filled with excitement and shouts, and occasionally it plummets down, leaving everyone screaming (except seasoned investors, who know it'll swing back up again). These ups and downs are called trends, and charting lets us detect them like a hawk poised on a mountainside.

But wait, how do we notice these trends? That's where our two dependable tools come in: candlesticks and trend lines.

- Candlesticks: Think of them as tiny miniature troops standing shoulder-to-shoulder on the chart. Each candlestick offers a tale about what transpired in the market over a given period, generally a day. They have four parts:

- The body: This colored rectangle indicates the opening and closing prices. Green signifies the price increased, and red means it went down. Easy, right?

- The wicks: Those thin lines protruding out above and below the body are called wicks. They reflect the top and lowest prices attained throughout that time. Long wicks might be a symptom of uncertainty or instability.

- The shadow: The colorful area of the wick is called the shadow. A lengthy lower shadow on a green candle might imply buyers jumped in to stop the price from dropping further.

Now, let's learn to understand the language of candlesticks:

- Long green bodies: Happy warriors marching up! The price is growing steadily.
- Short green bodies with lengthy upper wicks: Bullish indecision. Buyers drove the price up, while some sellers sought to drive it down.
- Long red bodies: Uh oh, the bears are out! The price is plummeting dramatically.
- Short red bodies with extended lower wicks: Buyers bravely attempt to stop the price from sinking further.
- Trend lines: These are like magic markers painted over the chart, linking important highs or lows. They assist us in seeing the general direction of the market. There are two primary types:

- Upward trend line: Connects consecutive higher lows, showing the price is typically increasing.
- Downward trend line: Connects consecutive lower highs, showing the price is typically dropping.

But remember, trend lines aren't barriers! They may be broken, signaling a probable shift in direction. That's why it's crucial to utilize them with other tools and not depend completely on them.

Now, let's put our newfound charting talents to the test! Imagine you're looking at a chart of your favorite crypto, let's call it ChocoCoin. You observe a group of green candles with lengthy bodies, producing a gorgeous rising trend line. This might be a positive indication! ChocoCoin could be on the rise, and you might consider purchasing some.

But wait, suddenly, you see a long red candle burst through the trend line! Uh my, it may be a warning sign. ChocoCoin could be headed down. It's time to be cautious and maybe wait for confirmation before making any choices.

Remember, charting is a great tool, but it's not a crystal ball. Use it together with other aspects like news, analysis, and your gut feeling to make educated judgments.

Here are some suggestions for mastering charting:

- Start simple: Don't overload yourself with sophisticated indicators. Focus on learning candlesticks and trend lines first.
- Practice makes perfect: The more charts you evaluate, the better you'll get at recognizing patterns.
- Don't pursue trends: Just because a price is going up doesn't indicate it will keep going up forever. Remember, trends may reverse.
- Set reasonable expectations: Charting can't foretell the future with accuracy. It's a tool to help you make smarter choices, not assurances of success.

So, young investors, keep discovering the world of charting! Remember, information is power, and knowing the market's language will give you an advantage in your crypto adventures. Now go out, get your markers, and conquer those charts!

Bonus Activity: Find a real-time crypto chart and practice spotting candlesticks and trend lines. Share your insight with others and see if you can forecast the next move!

Remember, always trade responsibly and with the advice of a competent adult.

Happy charting, future crypto lords!

Chapter Seven

Unveiling the Crypto Exchange's Hidden Marketplace

Welcome back, little crypto adventurers! We've grasped the fundamentals of buying, selling, and trading jargon. Now, it's time to plunge into the heart of any crypto exchange: the Order Book! Imagine it as a mystical marketplace where buyers and sellers whisper their desires to each other, secretly haggling over the price of their favorite coins. Sounds strange, right? Don't worry, we'll break its code together!

Picture a large whiteboard, teeming with colorful sticky notes. On one side, buyers (in green) indicate their preferred pricing and how much they're prepared to pay for a certain coin. These are termed "bids." On the opposite side, sellers (in red) push up their asking prices, hoping to find someone prepared to match their demands. These are termed "asks."

Think of bids as "I want to buy" notes and questions as "I want to sell" notes. The closer the bids and requests become, the hotter the negotiation! If a buyer's bid meets a seller's ask, bingo! An exchange occurs, and both parties walk away satisfied with their glittering new coins or crisp banknotes.

But here's the twist: the order book isn't simply a random mass of notes. It's structured like a neatly stacked ladder, with the highest bids at the top and the lowest requests at the bottom. This ladder is called the "depth chart," and it tells you how much demand or supply there is at various price points.

Think of the depth chart as a popularity contest for pricing. The more bids or asks at a specific price, the thicker the ladder rung at that point. A thick rung for bids suggests many buyers are ready to purchase at that price, while a thick rung for asks means many sellers are prepared to sell at that price.

Now, let's see how this plays out in real life:

Scenario 1: You're a ravenous pizza lover, and Bitcoin is the additional pepperoni. You badly want some Bitcoin, so you submit a hefty offer expecting to take it up immediately. But regrettably, there are no vendors prepared to let go at your price yet. Your bid rests at the top of the ladder, waiting for an eager seller to climb down and meet your offer.

Scenario 2: You're a giving person with more Bitcoin than you need. You decide to sell some to get that fantastic new skateboard. You post an ask at a good price, hoping for a speedy sale. But wait! There are already other vendors asking for considerably less. Your ask is moved down the ladder, waiting for a buyer eager to step up and pay your price.

The order book is continuously changing, like a swarm of digital butterflies fluttering their pricing. As deals happen, notes vanish and new ones show up, keeping the marketplace bustling with activity. By knowing how bids and asks operate and reading the depth chart, you can make educated judgments about whether to purchase or sell and become a skilled crypto trader!

Here are some helpful suggestions for exploring the order book:

- Start small: Don't jump in with huge orders immediately away. Place tiny test transactions to gain a sense of the market and how fast your orders are completed.
- Be patient: Don't expect your order to be completed promptly, particularly if it's distant from the current market price. The closer your bid or ask is to the current price, the sooner it will likely be filled.
- Keep an eye on the depth chart: Watch how the ladder evolves. A rapid surge in bids or offers at a specific price might suggest a shift in market sentiment.

- Use limit orders: These enable you to designate the precise price you're prepared to purchase or sell at, giving you greater control over your transactions.

Remember, the order book is your buddy! By learning its secrets, you may unleash the actual potential of crypto trading and become a master of the digital economy. Now go out, little Padawan, and conquer the charts!

Bonus Challenge: Try your hand at replicating the order book with real-time market data! Many internet platforms provide order book representations and practice trading options. Remember, always start with tiny, simulated transactions before moving into the actual market.

With experience and patience, you'll be navigating the order book like an expert in no time! Happy trading!

Chapter Eight

Trading Tools & Tricks: Conquering the Crypto Market with Smart Orders

Welcome back, small giants of the crypto trading world! Now that you've learned the fundamentals of buying, selling, and monitoring those charts like a hawk, it's time to unlock some extremely awesome trading tools that will make you a genuine market maestro. These are like hidden weapons in your trading armory, letting you traverse the crypto waves with accuracy and confidence.

So, put on your thinking hats, grab your imagined laser swords (because crypto trading is great!), and be ready to conquer the market with these smart tricks:

- Limit Orders: Imagine you're at a candy store, but instead of grabbing the first lollipop you see, you tell the proprietor your specific pricing and taste desire. That's what a limit order is! You establish a specified price at which you wish to purchase or sell a certain quantity of crypto, and your order only gets executed if the market hits that price point. This is ideal for:

- Snagging bargains: See a potential coin dropping in price? Set a limit order below the current price, and if it falls that low, bang! You've got some digital treasure at a bargain.

- Making smart moves: Do you have a feeling about a coin breaking past a barrier level? Set a limit order slightly above that level, and if your forecast comes true, you may gain on the rising trend.

- Avoid panic-selling: Sometimes, the market might become a bit unstable. But before selling in a frenzy, use limit orders at critical support levels to safeguard your gains if things become too heated.

- Stop-Loss Orders: Think of this as your reliable market-calming shield. A stop-loss order directs the exchange to automatically sell your crypto if the price falls below a particular value you select. It's like having a virtual bodyguard who says, "Hold on, champ, things are getting dicey, let's cash out before things get worse." This is vital for:

- Limiting your losses: No one loves watching their crypto assets dwindle, but occasionally, even the best-laid plans go astray. Setting stop-loss orders helps you reduce possible losses and safeguard your valuable crypto investment.

- Safeguarding profits: Had a fortunate run and your crypto is soaring? Set a stop-loss order a little below the current price to lock in some gains, even if the market takes a fall.

- Peace of mind: Knowing you have a safety net in place might help you sleep easily at night, without continually checking the charts and worrying about price swings.

- Market Buys: Now, for some fast enjoyment! Unlike the patient approach of limit orders, market buys are all about snatching up crypto as fast as possible, at whatever the current price is. Think of it like racing to the head of the line at a concert to snag the best position. This is ideal for:

- Capitalizing on unexpected opportunities: See a flash collapse or a breakthrough rally? A market purchase enables you to step in right immediately and perhaps snag some precious crypto before the price soars up.

- Reacting to major events: Big news may drive the market into a frenzy. Use market buys to immediately position yourself if you feel the news will favorably influence your selected currencies.

- Short-term trades: If you're aiming to purchase and sell fast to profit on modest price swings, market buys might be your go-to.

- Combining the Weapons: Remember, these instruments are most potent when utilized intelligently. You may blend them as a master chef combines ingredients to make the ultimate trading dish. For example, you may construct a limit order to purchase a dip with a stop-loss order below it to reduce possible losses. Or, you may utilize a market buy to join a fast-rising market followed by a limit order to lock in winnings later.

Remember, practice makes perfect! Experiment with these tools in a virtual trading environment or with tiny amounts of actual crypto to become familiar. The more you play around, the more you'll grasp how each tool works and how to utilize them to your advantage.

Trading is a marathon, not a sprint. Patience, discipline, and a strong grasp of these helpful tools will make you a well-equipped investor, ready to surf the crypto waves with confidence and expertise. So, go out, young titans, and rule the market with your newfound talents! Just remember, always trade responsibly, observe the regulations, and never spend more than you can afford to lose.

Bonus Tip: Keep a trading notebook to log your transactions, the tools you used, and the outcomes. This will let you examine your performance, learn from your errors, and optimize your trading techniques over time.

With these tools and your passion for knowledge, the crypto cosmos is your oyster! Go out and unleash your inner trading champion!

Part Three :
Investing Smarts for
Young Sharks

Chapter Nine

Time Travel with Crypto: The Compounding Magic that Grows Your Fortune

Imagine a miracle medicine that grows your money, not instantly, but consistently over time. No, it's not alchemy, it's the astonishing power of compounding! In the realm of crypto, compounding may be your hidden weapon, converting even little sums into a treasure trove over the years.

Buckle up, young investors, because we're about to go on a time-traveling expedition to observe how compounding works its magic!

The Compound Effect: A Snowball Rolling Downhill

Think of compounding as a snowball sliding down a snowy slope. It begins little, maybe just a handful of soft snow. But with each roll, it scoops up more and more snow, becoming larger and heavier until it forms a massive snowball you can scarcely push! That's how compounding works with your Bitcoin.

Every piece of interest you earn doesn't simply evaporate, it gets added to your original investment, and then you receive interest on that higher amount too. It's like a snowball effect, helping your crypto holdings grow greater and quicker over time.

The Time Machine Factor: Patience is Key

But here's the key element that makes compounding magical: time. The longer you let your crypto sit and "compound," the greater the snowball grows. Imagine putting part of your Saturday lemonade stand profits in Bitcoin when you're 10 years old. If you keep onto it and let the interest build up for 10 years, you could be shocked at how much it's grown by the time you're 20! It's like your crypto has been going through a time machine, growing discreetly in the background as you go about your amazing child activities.

The Power of Small Beginnings: Don't Underestimate Your Piggy Bank

Don't worry if your crypto treasure isn't as enormous as a dragon's hoard yet. Even modest sums may perform wonders with compounding. Remember, that snowball began as just a little scoop of snow! The main thing is to begin early and allow the magic of time to work its miracles. Even beginning with a few dollars or naira from your piggy bank may make a great impact in the long term. Think of it like planting a seed, the sooner you plant, the higher and stronger the tree will grow.

The Compound Caveat: Risks and Responsibilities

Of course, like any excursion, there are things to bear in mind. Crypto markets may be volatile, meaning prices can move up and down rapidly. So, although compounding may be tremendous, it's crucial to recognize the dangers and invest properly. Always do your homework, speak to your parents or guardians, and only invest what you can afford to lose. Remember, patience and understanding are your greatest allies on this time-traveling voyage.

Ready to Set Your Crypto on Autopilot?

The beauty of compounding is that it works even while you sleep! Once you've invested, you can sit back, relax, and allow the power of time and interest to do its job. Of course, keep an eye on the market and be educated, but don't get caught up in day-to-day changes. Trust the long-term magic of compounding, and you could just be amazed at the treasure trove you've amassed by the time you reach maturity.

Remember, young investors:

- Start early: The sooner you start compounding, the more time your bitcoin has to grow.

- Be patient: Compounding is a marathon, not a sprint. Give it time to perform its magic.

- Invest responsibly: Only invest what you can afford to lose, and do your homework before investing your money in any crypto.

- Enjoy the ride!: Learning about investing and seeing your crypto develop can be a fascinating and rewarding activity.

So, are you ready to unleash the magic of compounding and take your crypto on a time-traveling journey? Remember, the future is yours to construct, and with a little patience and the miracle of compounding, you can develop a financial kingdom worthy of any young investor!

Bonus Tip: Check out these online compound interest calculators to see how your Bitcoin may increase over time. It's a great way to see the power of compounding and feel enthusiastic about your financial future!

I hope this chapter has given you a clearer understanding of the remarkable power of compounding and how it may help you build your crypto assets over time. Remember, the future is full of possibilities, and with the appropriate information and a little patience, you can do everything you put your mind to. Now go out, young investors, and conquer the world of crypto with the power of compounding at your side!

Chapter Ten

Building a Balanced Portfolio: Diversification for Young Crypto Champs

Remember that fantastic Pokémon team you built? The one with Pikachu for power, Bulbasaur for defense, and Squirtle for...well, simply because Squirtle is awesome? Building a crypto portfolio is somewhat like establishing that great squad - you need diversification to face diverse assaults and win the market game!

Just as you wouldn't depend only on Charmander to face a water-type Pokémon, you shouldn't put all your allowance in just one cryptocurrency. Why? Because the crypto world is chaotic, and unpredictable, and often throws curveballs like Pikachu squaring off against a Machamp. One coin could rise, while another might suddenly perform a Snorlax and fall asleep (metaphorically speaking, of course!).

The Diversification Power Play:
Diversification is your best protection against market fluctuations. It's like having a team of Pokémon ready for any fight. By diversifying your assets among several sorts of cryptocurrencies, you're effectively establishing a safety net. If one of your coins tumbles like a Magikarp, the others may stand firm and maybe even carry the day.

Crypto Categories: Your Diverse Squad:

Now, you may be asking, "Which Pokémon, I mean, cryptos, should I add to my team?" Don't worry, young investor, here's an overview of the basic varieties you can pick from:

- The Blue Chips: These are the Bitcoin and Ethereums of the crypto world - the steady veterans with established track records. They may not promise rapid development, but they're like your faithful Charizard, always trustworthy and ready to unleash a Flamethrower when required.

- The Rising Stars: Think of them as your Eevee evolutions - coins with enormous potential for development. Maybe it's a new initiative tackling an interesting issue or a rising star in a certain crypto sector. Just remember, tremendous potential also equals increased danger, so walk cautiously like approaching a Scyther for the first time.

- The Utility Players: These are the Mr. Mimes of the crypto world - they may not be the flashiest, but they have specialized applications like running decentralized apps or conducting online payments. These may be fantastic long-term investments, with Bulbasaur gradually sprouting vines of value.

- The Stablecoins: Imagine them as your Snorlaxes — they're tied to real-world assets like the dollar, bringing stability to the often tumultuous crypto market. Think of them as your haven, a place to put your crypto when the market begins looking like a Gyarados on a rampage.

Building Your Crypto Team:

Remember, establishing a balanced portfolio is like mixing a smoothie. You wouldn't simply put in bananas and mangoes, right? You need a variety of tastes and textures to make it enjoyable and healthful. Similarly, your crypto team shouldn't be just Bitcoin or simply odd cryptocurrencies you noticed trending on Twitter.

Here are some ideas for developing a balanced portfolio:

- Know your risk tolerance: Are you a Pikachu, comfortable with little but consistent gains? Or are you a Charizard, determined to seek big profits even if it means confronting dangers like battling a Dragonite? Knowing your risk appetite will help you find the correct combination of reliable and risky coins.

- Do your research: Don't simply blindly invest in something your cousin's friend's uncle's dog read about online. Research each coin, learn its function, and appraise its potential. Think of it like researching your opponent before a Pokémon fight!

- Start small and diversify: You don't need a million Pokédollars to start investing. Begin with a tiny amount and disperse it among several categories. Remember, even Bulbasaur may develop into a formidable Venusaur with time and care.

- Rebalance regularly: Just as your Pokémon team can require modifications as you advance in the game, your Bitcoin portfolio might need alterations too. Keep an eye on your assets and rebalance frequently to maintain your preferred level of risk and possible profits.

Remember, diversification is not about avoiding risk, it's about managing it. By constructing a diversified portfolio, you're giving yourself the greatest opportunity to navigate the fascinating, yet often unexpected, world of cryptocurrencies. So go out, young investors, form your winning crypto squad, and remember, even if you face a Legendary Pokémon like Mewtwo, with a little study and diversity, you can become the Crypto Master of your financial destiny!

Bonus Tip: Talk to your parents or responsible people about developing your crypto holdings. They can assist you in managing the complexity of the market and make informed financial selections. Remember, even the strongest Pokémon trainers need assistance from Professor Oak occasionally!

And that's a wrap on establishing your portfolio, young crypto champions! Go out and diversify.

Chapter Eleven

Crypto & the Real World: Bridging the Digital and Physical

Welcome back, little crypto adventurers! We've conquered the basics of trading, unlocked the secrets of smart investments, and even become responsible digital citizens. But our journey doesn't end there. It's time to bridge the gap between the exciting world of crypto and the real world you navigate every day.

Let's see how these digital coins can interact with traditional finance and even fuel your everyday purchases!

Crypto and Traditional Finance: A Handshake or a High Five?

Imagine two worlds, one bustling with digital assets like Bitcoin and Ethereum, the other operating with familiar paper bills and bank accounts. These two worlds, crypto, and traditional finance, co-exist but haven't quite figured out the dance moves for a perfect tango.

Here's how things stand:

- Investing with a Crypto Twist: You can now invest in traditional stocks and bonds using cryptocurrency! Some platforms allow you to buy shares of real-world companies like Tesla or Apple with your Bitcoin or Ethereum. This opens up new investment opportunities and blurs the lines between the two worlds.

- Loans with a Digital Touch: Need a loan but don't have enough cash? Some lenders are starting to accept crypto as collateral. This means you can use your digital assets to secure a loan for, say, buying a car or starting a business. But remember, borrowing comes with risks, so always tread carefully!

- Payments in the Digital Age: While not yet mainstream, some forward-thinking companies are accepting cryptocurrency as payment for goods and services. Imagine buying your favorite video game or grabbing a pizza with Bitcoin! This trend is still in its early stages, but it holds exciting possibilities for the future of commerce.

However, this handshake between crypto and traditional finance isn't without its bumps. Regulations are still evolving, and there are concerns about volatility and security. But remember, innovation rarely happens smoothly – think of the bumpy ride from horse-drawn carriages to self-driving cars!

Crypto in Your Backpack: Everyday Purchases with Digital Coins

Now, let's get down to the nitty-gritty: how can you use crypto for everyday purchases like that cool new skateboard or the latest sneakers? While widespread adoption is still on the horizon, here are some glimpses of the future:

☐ Gift Cards with a Crypto Kick: Some companies offer gift cards that can be purchased with cryptocurrency and redeemed at popular retailers. This lets you tap into the crypto world for everyday shopping.

☐ Peer-to-Peer Payments: Sending money to friends or family across borders just got easier and faster with crypto. Platforms like Bitcoin Lightning Network enable instant and cheap transactions, making traditional money transfers seem like snail mail!

☐ Loyalty Programs with a Digital Edge: Imagine earning crypto rewards for your everyday purchases! Some stores and platforms are experimenting with crypto-based loyalty programs, giving you an extra incentive to use your digital coins.

Remember, the real-world applications of crypto are still in their early stages. But just like the first clunky computers eventually led to sleek laptops and smartphones, the possibilities for crypto in everyday life are vast and exciting!

The Future of Finance: A Crypto Cocktail?

So, will crypto completely replace traditional finance one day? Probably not. More likely, the two worlds will continue to evolve and intertwine, creating a hybrid financial system that benefits from the strengths of both. Imagine a future where you can seamlessly switch between using your local currency and your favorite cryptocurrency, depending on the situation. Pretty cool, right?

As young crypto pioneers, you have the opportunity to shape this future. By understanding how crypto interacts with the real world, you can make informed decisions, explore new possibilities, and contribute to building a more inclusive and innovative financial system.

Remember, young crypto explorers:
The crypto world is still evolving, so keep learning and stay informed.
Be cautious and responsible when using crypto for real-world purchases.
Don't be afraid to explore and experiment, but always do your research before taking any risks.

The future of finance is a blank canvas, and you hold the brush. So, let's paint a world where crypto empowers you, fuels your dreams, and makes everyday life a little more exciting!

Dive Deeper!

- ☐ Research companies and platforms that offer crypto-related services like investments, loans, and payments.
- ☐ Explore the concept of stablecoins, which are cryptocurrencies designed to peg their value to traditional assets like the US dollar.
- ☐ Discuss with your family and friends how you see crypto playing a role in your future financial life.

Chapter Twelve

Responsible Crypto Citizen

Cracking the Security Code and Avoiding Cryptocurrency Calamities

Hold onto your rockets, young crypto cadets! Before you blast off into the exciting world of trading and investing, let's buckle up with some essential safety gear. Being a responsible crypto citizen might sound boring, but trust us, it's like wearing a virtual spacesuit, protecting you from sneaky space pirates and ensuring your financial fuel tank doesn't get punctured.

So, put on your thinking caps and get ready to become a champion of cybersecurity, responsible trading, and scam-busting!

Cybersecurity 101: Keeping Your Coins In Your Castle

Imagine your crypto stash as a treasure chest overflowing with golden Bitcoin bars. Keeping those bars safe requires building a virtual fortress, and here's how:

- Password Power Plant: Treat your passwords like magical keys to your castle. Make them strong, unique, and kept secret, like a ninja hiding in the shadows. Never share them with anyone, not even your best robo-dog!

- Two-Factor Fortress: Think of two-factor authentication (2FA) as a drawbridge with a grumpy troll guarding it. Even if someone steals your key, they'll need the troll's magic potion (one-time code) to enter. Set it up on every crypto account you have, making your castle virtually impenetrable.

- Software Shield: Don't click on shady links or download suspicious apps! They could be traps set by sneaky scammers trying to steal your coins. Only use trusted software and websites recommended by your parents or crypto mentors.

- Backup Bunker: Imagine losing your castle key! That's what happens if you lose your crypto wallet information. Always back up your private keys and seed phrases in a safe place, like a fireproof piggy bank for digital treasures. Remember, no one, not even the Queen of

Crypto herself, can recover your coins if you lose those keys!

Trading Like a Titan: Responsible Habits for Crypto Champions

Being a responsible crypto trader means making smart choices, just like a wise investor planning for their future space yacht. Here are some golden rules:

- Plan Your Pirate Plunder: Set goals and create a budget for your crypto adventures. Don't spend more than you can afford to lose, just like your parents budget for groceries (and, hopefully, treats!).

- Research Rocket Fuel: Before investing in any crypto, do your research! Read articles, watch educational videos, and ask your parents and mentors for advice. Think of it like exploring a new planet before landing your spaceship.

- Don't Panic, Captain Cool: The crypto market may be like a turbulent rollercoaster ride. Stay cool and avoid making rash judgments based on dramatic price fluctuations. Remember, patience is a superpower!

- Diversify Your Asteroid Field: Don't put all your eggs in one basket! Spread your assets among several forms of crypto (like having a selection of fruit in your lunchbox) to reduce risk.

- Know When to Fold 'Em: Sometimes, the greatest trade is no trade at all. If an investment doesn't seem right, don't be scared to cut your losses and go on. Think of it like navigating your spacecraft away from a meteor shower.

Scam Squad Busters: Spotting Crafty Crypto Crooks

Just as superheroes combat villains, responsible crypto citizens need to be on the watch for deceptive fraudsters. Here are some red signs to look out for:

- Get-Rich-Quick Schemes: If someone offers assured, overnight riches with Bitcoin, run faster than a rocket with a flat tire! These are usually always scams.

- Too-Good-to-Be-True Deals: If someone gives you free Bitcoins or quadruples your money in a flash, it's a trap! Remember, nothing good comes easily, particularly in the digital age.

- Phishing Pirates: These fraudsters send bogus emails or texts purporting to be from reputable crypto firms. They aim to deceive you into disclosing your personal information or clicking on dangerous websites. Be aware of anything that appears strange and always double-check the sender's information before clicking anything.

- Pump-and-Dump Plots: Scammers could artificially increase the price of a useless coin and then sell it when others buy in, leaving you clutching an empty spacecraft fuel tank. Research and investments before hopping on board the hype train.

Remember, the greatest protection against fraud is education and prudence. Keep your head up, and your defence strong, and always seek aid if anything seems weird. Together, we can maintain the crypto ecosystem secure and attractive for young investors like you!

Become a Crypto Crusader!

Spread the word about ethical crypto citizenship! Share your expertise with your friends, family, and classmates. Educate them about cybersecurity, safe trading, and recognizing frauds. Together, you may develop a robust community of young crypto enthusiasts.

Part Four : Bonus Level: Advanced Adventures

Chapter Thirteen

Beyond Exchanges: Exploring Advanced Adventures

You've learned the fundamentals of trading, developed a respectable crypto portfolio, and even dabbled in some rudimentary analysis. Now, it's time to pry open the treasure vault of difficult crypto adventures!

This chapter is your introduction to intriguing new realms like Decentralized Finance (DeFi), Non-Fungible Tokens (NFTs), and the ever-evolving crypto environment. Buckle up, young investors, because things are about to become much more fascinating!

DeFi: Where Crypto Takes the Wheel

Forget centralized banks and flashy suits. Imagine a financial system driven by code, managed by algorithms, and available to anybody with an internet connection. That's DeFi, essentially — a whole new playground where you may borrow, lend, earn interest, and even trade without depending on conventional institutions. But how does it work?

Think of DeFi as a set of smart contracts, like small robots on the blockchain, programmed to obey certain rules. You deposit your crypto into these contracts, and they automatically perform activities depending on the code. Want to lend your Bitcoin and earn interest? There's a DeFi project for that! Need to borrow enough Ethereum to purchase that limited-edition NFT?

Another contract may assist! It's like establishing your private bank, available 24/7 and controlled by robotic assistants.

Of course, stepping inside DeFi demands additional care. It's like exploring a forest, thrilling, full of possibility, but also riddled with hidden perils. Before plunging in, make sure you understand the hazards, use reliable sites, and always do your homework. Remember, your crypto is your responsibility, so walk cautiously and learn as you go!

NFTs: Owning More Than Just Bits and Bytes

Have you ever desired to acquire a piece of your favorite artist's work, but without the high price tag or the necessity for a costly museum? That's where NFTs come in, unique digital tokens that signify ownership of everything from artwork and music to in-game objects and even your online persona. Think of them as digital certificates of authenticity for your virtual possessions.

NFTs are kept on the blockchain, making them hard to falsify or copy. Want to sell your unique digital joke for a pixelated spaceship? No problem! The NFT economy is flourishing, with artists and collectors joining together to purchase, sell, and appreciate unique digital products.

But NFTs aren't only about buying and selling. They're opening up new methods to support artists directly, access unique experiences, and even establish virtual communities around common passions. Imagine buying a piece of music that gets you access to an exclusive artist community, or an NFT that lets you vote on choices in a decentralized game. The options are infinite!

The Crypto Universe Keeps Evolving

The world of crypto is like a live, breathing creature, continuously evolving and developing. New initiatives, technologies, and applications are cropping up every day, pushing the frontiers of what's possible. Staying ahead of the curve is part of the fun, so keep your eyes open for interesting advancements like:

- ☐ Central Bank Digital Currencies (CBDCs): Governments are researching their digital currencies, which might one day compete with or perhaps replace conventional money.

☐ Metaverse Integration: Virtual worlds where you may spend, invest, and even own virtual land are becoming more popular, blurring the barriers between the actual and digital worlds.

☐ Gaming Meets Crypto: Play-to-earn games are revolutionizing the way we engage with video games, enabling players to earn crypto prizes and even own in-game assets.

Be Bold, Be Curious, Be Responsible

As you journey into these sophisticated areas, remember to always keep a healthy dosage of caution and curiosity. Do your study, ask questions, and never be hesitant to explore. The future of finance is being defined by inventive minds like yours, so keep trying, learning, and pushing the limits of what's possible. Just remember, with tremendous power comes great responsibility. As young investors, you have the chance to influence the future of crypto and make it a force for good in the world. Use your information intelligently, invest safely, and constantly aim to contribute to a more decentralized and inclusive financial system for everyone.

Chapter Fourteen

The Future of Finance: Shaping Today and Tomorrow

Imagine a future where money flows freely across borders, available to anybody with a smartphone. Where financial choices are determined by algorithms, not faceless businesses. Where ownership is clear and trust is founded on code, not papers. This, young investors, is the possible future of finance, and you can influence it.

Cryptocurrency is more than simply a new asset class. It's a technology revolution with the potential to revolutionize how we save, invest, and interact with money. Think of it as a blank canvas, ready for a generation of young, tech-savvy brains to create a masterpiece of financial inclusion and innovation.

But what does this future hold for you, specifically? How can you, as young investors, become active players in defining this exciting new landscape? Here are a few ways you can make a difference:

1. Be an educated investor: Knowledge is power in the crypto world. Keep learning about new technology, initiatives, and trends. Stay interested, ask questions, and don't be hesitant to challenge the established quo.

2. Support creative initiatives: Invest in crypto firms and projects that coincide with your ideals, whether it's advancing decentralized finance,

sustainability, or ethical practices. Your investments may convey a strong statement about the sort of future you wish to see.

3. Advocate for responsible development: Cryptocurrency has a dark side, with concerns including environmental effects, scams, and security risks. Speak out against harmful practices, support safe and responsible innovation, and hold the industry accountable for its activities.

4. Join the community: Connect with other young investors, entrepreneurs, and developers in the crypto field. Share your ideas, learn from others, and cooperate on initiatives to create a better future together.

5. Lead by example: Show the world that young people can be responsible, knowledgeable, and effective investors in the crypto revolution. Be a role model for others, and motivate them to join the struggle for a more inclusive and fair financial system.

Remember, the future of finance isn't etched in stone. It's a tale that's always being written, and every one of you has a pen in your hand. So, seize it, be brave, be creative, and create a chapter that helps everyone. The world is watching, and your voice matters.

As we end this chapter on your crypto adventure, remember that the trip is only starting. The world of finance is evolving quickly, and you have the chance to be at the vanguard of that transformation. Embrace the difficulties, seize on the chances, and constantly try to make your imprint on the future. Who knows, in a few years, you may be the one educating others about the wonderful world of crypto - a world formed by your curiosity, daring, and devotion. Now go out, young investors, and establish a better financial future for yourself and the planet!

Conclusion

Your Crypto Odyssey Begins Now

Congratulations, little crypto adventurer! You've sailed the thrilling beaches of trading, constructed a robust investment ship, and traveled into the undiscovered seas of DeFi, NFTs, and the ever-evolving crypto environment. Now, it's time to send your sails towards the wide horizon of the future, where your knowledge and talents will lead you in constructing a new financial world.

Remember the essential lessons from this journey:

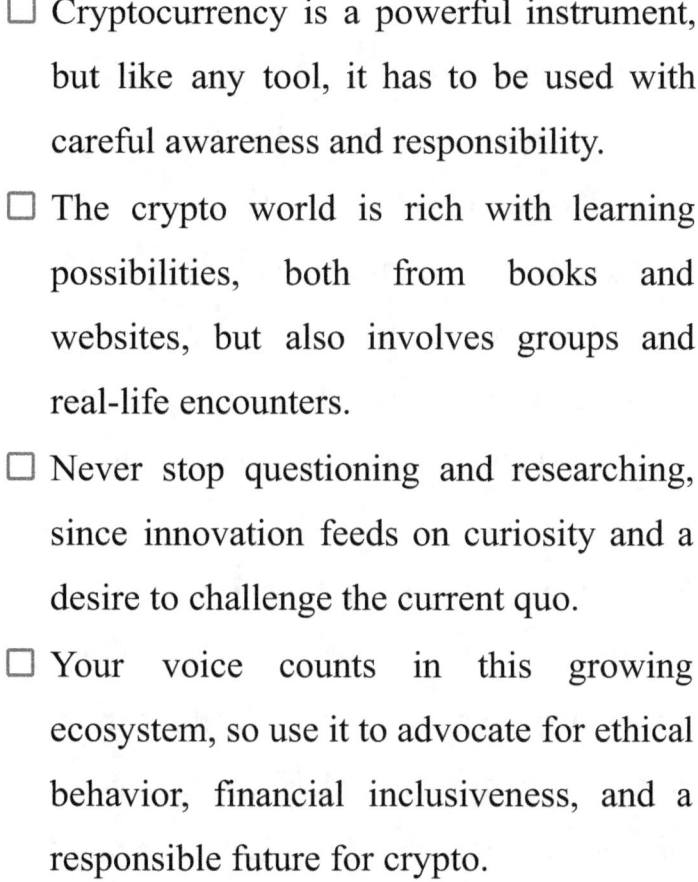

☐ Cryptocurrency is a powerful instrument, but like any tool, it has to be used with careful awareness and responsibility.

☐ The crypto world is rich with learning possibilities, both from books and websites, but also involves groups and real-life encounters.

☐ Never stop questioning and researching, since innovation feeds on curiosity and a desire to challenge the current quo.

☐ Your voice counts in this growing ecosystem, so use it to advocate for ethical behavior, financial inclusiveness, and a responsible future for crypto.

As you navigate your future financial adventures, here are some tools to keep your compass steady:

- Educational websites: CoinGecko, CoinMarketCap, Binance Academy, Kraken Learn
- Crypto communities: Reddit forums, Discord servers, online gatherings
- Events: Blockchain conferences, hackathons, educational seminars

Remember, you're not alone on this path. A community of young, enthusiastic investors stands with you, eager to learn, explore, and create a better financial future together. So, embrace the possibilities, keep your mind open, and never lose sight of the power you wield. The future of finance is yours to design, one brick at a time.

Go out, young investors, and let your crypto voyage begin! Remember, the most important treasure isn't found in a digital wallet, but in the knowledge, resilience, and enthusiasm you bring to every stage of your financial trip. So, map your path, set your sails, and explore the thrilling world of crypto with confidence and a grin. The future is waiting, and it's time to make it your own.